Publisher: Jeffrey Zeldman
Designer: Jason Santa Maria
Executive Director: Katel LeDû
Managing Editor: Tina Lee
Editor: Caren Litherland
Technical Editor: Jon Hicks
Copyeditor: Kate Towsey
Proofreader: Katel LeDû
Compositor: Ron Bilodeau
Ebook Producer: Ron Bilodeau

ISBN: 978-1-937557-57-7

A Book Apart
New York, New York
http://abookapart.com

TABLE OF CONTENTS

FOREWORD

RESOURCES ABOUND FOR PEOPLE who seek guidance on how to make the web more accessible. Many of those resources specifically cater to a developer audience: they offer techniques for creating semantically structured templates, keyboard accessible date pickers, or accordion widgets that work well with screen readers. We web professionals tend to love these resources for a couple of reasons. First, they make our products easier for people with disabilities to use; second, they allow us to work a little more quickly, without reinventing the wheel every time.

What we need more of, though, are books like Geri's. If you write the perfect code for a flawed design, you may end up with parts that still aren't accessible. In *Color Accessibility Workflows*, Geri effortlessly puts accessibility into the hands and mind of the designer.

Geri's approach to color on the web is inspiring, methodical, and pragmatic. She shares the science of color and vision, and offers details about the tools she uses to create accessible color schemes. Although she concentrates on design, she gets nerdy enough for the developers out there, too. And, perhaps most crucially, she shares her reasoning, decision-making, and tried-and-true process for working with color and accessibility. This book is so much more than just a reference on color. Web design and development techniques will forever come and go. Geri's focus on thinking and workflow ensures that this book will last.

—Derek Featherstone

INTRODUCTION

" In visual perception a color is almost never seen
as it really is—as it physically is. This fact makes
color the most relative medium in art."
—JOSEF ALBERS, Interaction of Color

The most talked-about dress in 2015 didn't appear on the red carpet; it surfaced as a viral photo that polarized the internet over whether it was white and gold, or blue and black. Although hypotheses abound about why the actual blue-and-black dress appeared to be white and gold for so many people, this seems beyond dispute: it all comes down to the perception of color.

German abstract painter Josef Albers, perhaps best remembered for his *Homage to the Square* paintings, was also a dedicated teacher who, in 1963, published an influential course on color theory that still has relevance today. He was right: color is relative—not just because it appears to differ across different surfaces, but also because it's seen differently by different people.

What comes to mind when you think of disabilities that affect how people interact with websites, apps, and video games? Maybe you think of physical disabilities that make traditional input devices, such as a mouse or game controller, impossible to use. Or maybe you think of a more extreme scenario, such as complete blindness, where a customer must rely on screen-reader technology to navigate the web. Or perhaps you think of the aging population, which finds small font sizes challenging to read.

Another disability, though, one that isn't talked about so often, affects a surprisingly large percentage of the population: color blindness. The so-called "Dressgate" phenomenon may have been a fun meme for plenty of people, but poor color perception is a frustrating part of many people's daily lives.

Compared to just a few decades ago, when most mass media was produced in black and white, color is increasingly used to impart information. Today, advances in technology allow us to view color everywhere—not just on television screens, comput-

**FIG 0:** Millions of colors surround us every day.

ers, and phones, but also in our cars, on our banking machines, appliances, and even watches—and the list goes on (**FIG 0**).

Color is a powerful tool that affords seemingly endless design possibilities, but far too many of us design with only one type of color vision in mind—our own. In this guide, we'll learn not only how to make accessible color choices, but also how to become better, more empathetic designers by discovering how other people see the world.

COLOR BLINDNESS

THE MISNOMER *color blindness* has led to false impressions about what someone affected by the condition experiences. Only in extremely rare instances does color blindness mean that a person can't see any color at all; *monochromacy* (also known as *achromatopsia*) affects an estimated one in forty thousand births worldwide. *Monochromats* experience not only a complete lack of color perception, but may have light sensitivity and reduced vision as well. By contrast, what most of us think of as "color blindness" is a very common condition referring to a decreased ability to see color, or a decreased ability to tell colors apart from one another (**FIG 1.1**). Because of this misconception, many people prefer to use the more accurate phrase *color vision deficiency* (CVD). Keeping this more nuanced understanding in mind, we'll use both terms throughout this book.

The majority of people who have color blindness inherit the condition as a genetic trait. This trait is more likely to occur in someone born chromosomally male (with XY chromosomes) than someone born chromosomally female (with XX chromosomes); the most common form of color blindness occurs in 8% of males, but in only 0.5% of females. Taken together, these statistics represent a significant portion of the population. We need to keep this demographic in mind as we work.

HOW COLOR BLINDNESS OCCURS

But first, let's grapple with the mechanics of color vision deficiency. Ready for some science?

Inside the human eye is a lining called the *retina*. The retina can be likened to a type of screen onto which an image is projected through other parts of the eye, including the pupil and lens (**FIG 1.2**).

Two types of photoreceptor cells, *rods* and *cones*, live inside the retina. Rods allow us to see dark and light, and shape and movement; cones allow us to perceive color. There are three types of cones, each containing a photopigment that is stimulated by red, green, or blue wavelengths in the spectrum. L-cones are sensitive to long wavelengths of light; M-cones are sensitive to medium wavelengths of light; and S-cones are

FIG 1.1: Top left: a person with normal color vision might see a website this way. Bottom right: how the same website might appear to a person with color blindness.

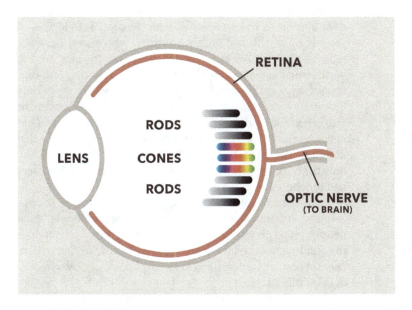

FIG 1.2: A diagram of the human eye.

sensitive to short wavelengths of light. When stimulated, the signals are combined in the brain and recognized as a color image—similar to how a computer mixes red, green, and blue light and emits it as an image on a screen.

Problems with color vision occur when one or more of these types of cones are defective or absent entirely. These problems can be inherited, or can be acquired through factors like trauma, exposure to ultraviolet light, degeneration with age, or as a side effect of diabetes.

People who have what is referred to as "normal" color vision are called *trichromats* because their color vision is based on all three types of healthy cones. In other words, they're capable of perceiving color detected from all three wavelengths of light. *Dichromats*, people who are missing an entire type of cone, can only perceive color detected from two wavelengths of light, a condition known as *dichromacy*.

Monochromacy is broken down into further distinctions. *Rod monochromacy*, the most severe condition, occurs when all three types of cones are faulty or missing and vision is dependent upon rods only, reducing color perception to shades of grey. People with rod monochromacy, who also experience reduced visual acuity and severe light sensitivity, may need to wear strong sunglasses both indoors and outdoors. *Blue-cone monochromacy*, a similarly severe condition, occurs when only blue cone receptors are functional. Blue-cone monochromats also experience reduced visual acuity and light sensitivity. *Cone monochromacy* is a less severe, extremely rare condition that does not affect visual acuity or light sensitivity. It occurs when only the red cone receptors or green cone receptors are present and functional.

To further complicate matters, a portion of one type of cone is faulty instead of completely absent in some people. Such people, called *anomalous trichromats*, have reduced sensitivities to color that may be less severe than what a dichromat experiences. They can be described as having a color *weakness* instead of color blindness.

Dr. Jay Neitz, a color vision researcher at the Medical College of Washington, states that trichromats with fully functional color vision can distinguish up to one million different colors, while a dichromat's palette is limited to just ten thousand colors. That's why dichromats are much more likely to be aware of their vision problem than anomalous trichromats, who might never know that they have mild color-defective vision unless they are tested.

WHAT COLOR BLINDNESS LOOKS LIKE

Have you ever noticed that it's much harder to discern color if you're in a dark space with no lighting? That's because our cones don't work as well in the dark; the rods are doing most of the work. Now imagine viewing the world this way under normal lighting conditions!

To convey what people with more severe types of color blindness experience, I'll focus on the different types of dichromacy. Remember that many people with deficiencies will see more colors than those shown in these simulated images, but not the full spectrum of color that most people with "normal" color vision see (FIG 1.3). Also note that because color blindness doesn't affect rod cells, people with color blindness can distinguish tones from light to dark (assuming they have no other vision problems).

Protanopia

Protanopia, or red-dichromacy, occurs when there's a total absence of L-cones. It's also one of the two types of color blindness commonly referred to as "red-green" color blindness. Affected people, called *protanopes*, have trouble distinguishing colors in the green–yellow–red area of the spectrum. In addition, the brightness of red, orange, and yellow colors is reduced. Reds often appear to be gray or black, and purples may be indistinguishable from shades of blue. A pink shirt, because it reflects both red and blue light, may simply appear blue. As the simulated images illustrate, the term "red-green" color blindness can be quite misleading, since protanopes often have trouble distinguishing many more colors beyond just red and green.

FIG 1.3: People with fully functional color vision are able to discern the full spectrum without significant confusion.

Protanopia-type deficiencies include *protanomaly*, a red-weakness, and together affect about 2% of chromosomal males (**FIG 1.4**).

Deuteranopia

Deuteranopia, or green-dichromacy, is the other "red-green" form of color blindness; it occurs when there's a total absence of M-cones. Affected people, called *deuteranopes*, have the same trouble distinguishing colors in the green–yellow–red area of the spectrum as protanopes do. Medium tones of red are more likely to be confused with oranges and yellows.

Deuteranomaly, a green-weakness, is by far the most common form of any color-vision deficiency, with roughly 5% of chromosomal males affected (**FIG 1.5**).

Tritanopia

Tritanopia is a much rarer form of color blindness. It is not inherited and is more likely to be acquired through old age, head injuries, or even alcoholism; it can potentially be reversed if the underlying cause is treated. Tritanopes, who lack S-cones, often confuse blue with green and yellow with violet.

FIG 1.4: People with severe protanopia have trouble distinguishing between reds, greens, and yellows. The brightness of colors may also be diminished.

FIG 1.5: People with severe deuteranopia also have trouble with reds, greens, and yellows, but brightness is generally unaffected.

Tritanopia and the related blue-weakness *tritanomaly* are not sex-linked traits, meaning they affect both chromosomal males and females equally. The number of people affected by tritanopia-type color blindnesses varies among different studies, but most say it occurs in less than 0.01% of the population (FIG 1.6).

FIG 1.6: People with severe tritanopia may confuse blue with green and yellow with violet.

TESTING FOR COLOR BLINDNESS

In the wake of 2015's viral "Dressgate" photo came an online test encouraging people to see if they belonged to "the 25% of the population" who are *tetrachromats*—that is, people born with an extra fourth cone who can potentially see up to one hundred million colors. As popular as the test was on social media, it was (perhaps not surprisingly) completely fake. While tetrachromacy is real, the condition in humans is so rare that the first scientifically confirmed case was only discovered in 2007. What's more, standard RGB computer monitors are incapable of displaying the range of colors required to accurately test for tetrachromacy—which raises questions about the accuracies of online vision testing in general.

Inaccurate, inconsistent color reproduction on home computer displays underscores the importance of getting properly tested for color blindness by a qualified vision specialist. Still, if you're curious, there are a few reputable online tests you might try on yourself. If they suggest you may be color-blind, it's best to follow up with a specialist for a confirmed medical diagnosis.

The most famous test is the Ishihara plate test, developed in 1916 and named after its creator, Dr. Shinobu Ishihara (FIG 1.7). The test consists of thirty-eight plates of numerals and lines hidden seamlessly within a field of dots. People who have

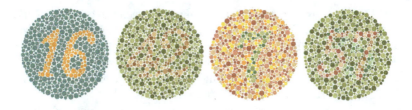

FIG 1.7: A selection of plates from the Ishihara color-blindness test.

trouble distinguishing the camouflaged numerals are known to have a color deficiency. Unfortunately, the test only evaluates forms of red-green color blindness, and even then with limited precision.

Alternatively, the Waggoner Computerized Color Vision Test (CCVT) is a paid test that provides more detailed information about which type of color blindness someone might have. The CCVT tests for protan, deutan, and tritan color vision deficiencies, and contains extra feedback about severity, if applicable.

HOW COLOR BLINDNESS AFFECTS PEOPLE

Although color blindness is surprisingly common, I had never met anybody who openly spoke about having the condition until I attended design school. Like many people with good color vision, I always took mine for granted; color blindness wasn't on my radar at all until my photography instructor, Ray Fennelly, opened up about it. As Ray recalled in an email conversation: "My design teacher, John Solowski, pointed it out to me in my first year at Ryerson University. I really was quite useless as a color printer. I guess that was why black-and-white photography appealed to me so much."

For my instructor, this meant he had to adapt to black-and-white photography—something he loved anyway—but for other people, being color-blind can have devastating effects on their career choices.

This may sound familiar if you've seen the 2006 film *Little Miss Sunshine*. Dwayne, the teenager who has taken a vow of silence until he fulfils his dream of becoming a test pilot, is horrified to discover he's color-blind; he realizes he'll never pass the screening test. Although the movie is fiction, this situation is a reality that many people have to face.

Screening tests are standard in many industries where color vision is a nonnegotiable requirement. Pilot, electrician, engineer, lab technician, and other career choices may simply be unattainable for those with color blindness. The topic is intensely debated by those who believe the concern is unwarranted. Many people feel discriminated against after failing vision tests when, in reality, they have no problem performing the job's day-to-day tasks.

In the United States, the Occupational Safety and Health Administration (OSHA) has no standards requiring normal color vision for any particular occupation; the standards are voluntary guidelines that are not regulated by federal or state government. Instead, each industry, employer, or vocational training program has final say about whether good color vision is a condition of employment, regardless of whether the person can perform the job functions safely or not.

This sort of prejudice abounds. In Japan, for example, color blindness has long been considered a disability for which affected people face widespread discrimination. The stigma derives from the publicity around a famous case within the Imperial Family. In 1920, the engagement of Hirohito, the eldest son of the Emperor of Japan, to Princess Nagako was vehemently opposed by Field Marshal Yamagata Aritomo, who alleged that Princess Nagako and her family were color-blind. He insisted that such a trait would damage the family's bloodlines, when in reality he wanted Hirohito to choose a bride from Yamagata's own clan instead. The effort to block the marriage failed (and it was proven that Princess Nagako was not color-blind at all), but the effect of perceiving color blindness as a negative trait persists in Japan today.

Yasuyo Takayanagi, an ophthalmologist and color-deficiency rights activist, conducted a survey in 1986 that revealed that nearly half of Japanese national universities discriminated against students and claimed that color-blind applicants were ineligible for admission "regardless of academic record." She states that although the number of universities observing this rule has decreased over the years, two national universities and one private university still retained the requirement as recently as 2014.

R-E-S-P-E-C-T

At this point you may be asking, "But we're just designing websites, right? Why does all this even matter?"

It's true that we may not have control over controversial rules and regulations in other industries. A designers and developers, though, we *do* have the ability to learn more about color blindness and make some simple changes to our workflows to mitigate the number of everyday frustrations faced by this significant demographic.

How often have you witnessed people who, attempting to use an app or website, blame themselves for being unable to comprehend or perform basic tasks? (Maybe *you've* even felt this way.) Too frequently, that feeling originates in design decisions that aren't the user's fault at all.

We have the capacity to make a website not just bare-minimum usable, but inclusive too—giving all readers the same confident, enjoyable experience, regardless of ability. This industry is ours, and we have the means—the obligation, even—to give all readers the respect they deserve.

Easier said than done, right? With so many businesses trying to take the easiest route from kickoff to launch day, it's clear that even essential accessibility is often not considered at all. Many well-meaning folks simply cannot understand the challenges faced by others unless they experience it themselves, and may not see the importance of baking in accessibility from the beginning. For those folks, making accessibility a business case will be a necessary tactic.

BAD FOR BUSINESS

If someone finds it frustrating to navigate your website, use your app, or play your game because of a color problem, they'll simply find an alternative. With nearly 5% of the overall population affected, it's easy to see how this can translate into lost readership and sales.

If that still isn't enough to convince a more adamant skeptic, it's important to understand that poor accessibility can quickly become an unexpected and very serious legal problem. Perhaps the most infamous case occurred in 2006, when the Maryland-based National Federation for the Blind (NFB) sued retailer Target Corporation for not addressing that Target.com was inaccessible to visually impaired users. In 2008, Target settled the class-action lawsuit, agreeing to pay class damages of $6 million and make the website fully accessible by February 2009, under the monitor of NFB themselves. Would you be prepared to face the consequences if your business was sued for creating a product or service that was unusable by a color-blind person?

So far, we've gone deep into the particulars of color blindness. We've learned what it is, how it affects people, and why it's absolutely essential to consider it in every project we build. With a solid understanding of this relative perception of color, it's time to learn how we can keep color accessibility in mind while assembling thoughtful color palettes.

2

CHOOSING
APPROPRIATE COLOR

WITH SEEMINGLY ENDLESS CHOICES, deciding on a color scheme for a project can feel like an overwhelming task for many designers. Although color psychology, message and meaning, and color harmony are beyond the scope of this book, this chapter will help define a starting point for choosing *appropriate* and *accessible* palettes.

COLOR FUNDAMENTALS

The ability to discriminate between colors relies on three attributes: hue, saturation, and lightness. Let's look at these elements more closely.

Hue

Hue is a color property. It's what we refer to when we say that something looks red, yellow, green, or blue—like the colors we perceive in a rainbow (FIG 2.1). This natural gradient from one hue to another can look quite different to a person with impaired vision, which is why simply choosing two hues, like red and blue, often won't provide enough contrast to be discernible.

Saturation

Saturation refers to the strength of a hue. The most saturated hue is the purest hue; the least saturated appears gray (FIG 2.2).

Lightness

Lightness (also called *brightness*) refers to the lightness or darkness of a color. It's produced by adding white or black. A *shade* is achieved by adding black to increase darkness; a *tint* is achieved by adding white to increase brightness. Many colors are in fact darker or lighter shades of others: browns are darker shades of orange; pinks are lighter tints of red (FIG 2.3).

FIG 2.1: A range of hues from red to violet.

FIG 2.2: Saturation progresses from a pure color to gray.

Shades   Tints

FIG 2.3: A range of dark green shades to bright green tints.

CONTRAST

As an illustrator, I know that one of the most important keys to a good painting is effective use of *contrast*. Contrast can take many forms: contrast of shape, contrast of color, contrast of texture, or contrast of scale, for example. These techniques can create emphasis and attract attention to the most important part of an artwork; when used with rhythm and composition, they can draw the eye to the next interesting area. In web design, the same techniques apply to create an easy-to-follow arrange-ment of information, keeping readers engaged and guiding them throughout the site. Aside from being a powerful means of achieving visual hierarchy, contrast is also one of the best ways to increase the readability of individual page elements, particularly text.

Unfortunately, a low-contrast design aesthetic suffuses the web (**FIG 2.4**). This minimalist trend has real consequences for our audiences. It can create unnecessary eye strain, make readers with even minor visual impairments feel "old" and incapable, and be completely illegible for more affected people. A conscious decision to choose low-contrast colors for the sake of aesthetics is simply unacceptable when usability plummets as a result.

The good news is that contrast can be easily achieved in numerous ways, some more effective than others. I'll outline a few of these methods.

Light-and-dark contrast

The most effective contrast occurs between light and dark colors. If you can, try not to use colors of a similar degree of lightness next to each other in a design (**FIG 2.5**).

Furthermore, since red-green color pairs (particularly when placed next to each other) cause problems for the majority of color-blind people, avoid such pairs if possible.

Complementary contrast

You can also achieve contrast by choosing complementary colors (except, of course, red and green), which appear opposite each other on a color wheel. Complementary color pairs generally work better than hues that are adjacent on the wheel. Again, remember to adjust lightness and darkness as required (**FIG 2.6**).

Warm-and-cool contrast

Contrast also exists between warm and cool colors on the color wheel (**FIG 2.7**). Effective use of warm-and-cool contrast appears in the works of skilled painters who understand the phenomenon of *atmospheric perspective*—objects in the distance appear

FIG 2.4: Some site designs prioritize style over legibility and readability, creating a challenge for readers with visual impairments.

Poor light and dark contrast · More effective light and dark contrast

FIG 2.5: The sampled red and green colors share a similar degree of lightness and don't provide enough contrast on their own without some adjustments.

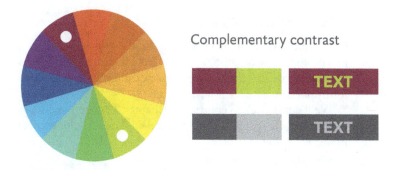

Complementary contrast

FIG 2.6: A complementary color pair can create more effective contrast than adjacent hues.

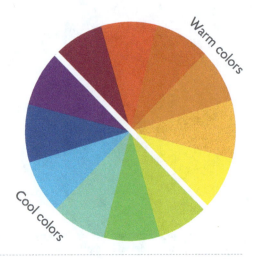

FIG 2.7: A color wheel divided into warm and cool colors.

Warm colors

Cool colors

to be cooler, while objects in the foreground appear to be warmer. A quick study of Leonardo da Vinci's *Mona Lisa*, for example, reveals that her hands—the closest point to the viewer—are the reddest and warmest, followed closely by the golden hues of her face, contrasted against the cool blue mountains of the background.

When designing with text, a dark shade of a cool color paired with a light tint of a warm color (**FIG 2.8**) provides better contrast than two warm colors or two cool colors (**FIG 2.9**).

Contrast of saturation

Contrast of saturation occurs when a dull color is placed next to a more intensely saturated color. Note that this technique is not as effective as light-and-dark contrast and should be avoided for important information (**FIG 2.10**).

We'll come back to contrast in Chapter 3, when we discuss how to achieve compliant contrast and implement color choices in our workflow.

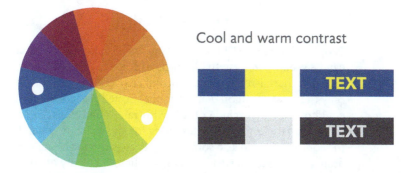

Cool and warm contrast

FIG 2.8: A dark shade of a cool color paired with a light tint of a warm color creates more effective contrast.

Warm contrast

FIG 2.9: A dark shade of a warm color paired with a light tint of a similar warm color creates less effective contrast.

Contrast of saturation

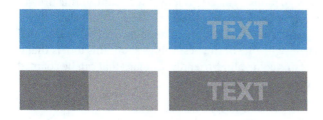

FIG 2.10: Placing a dull color next to a more saturated color is not recommended for creating effective contrast.

UNIVERSAL COLOR CHOICES

People often ask me if there are any "safe" color choices that can be seen by folks with all forms of color blindness. Unfortunately, there isn't a one-size-fits-all answer. Designing with only the most common deuteranopia-affected readers in mind could potentially exclude others with rarer conditions. Combined with the concerns of designing for low vision in general, the confusion could lead some designers to want to give up and design in grayscale instead! Of course, there are plenty of other ways to make color accessible without resorting to extremes, and there has been ample research and experimentation around which colors are most likely to be discernable by the greatest number of people.

The Japan-based *Color Universal Design Organization* (CUDO) developed a palette (PDF) containing colors that may be easier to discern individually by a more diverse color-blind audience. CUDO arrived at this palette by avoiding pure hues of red and green wherever possible; as a result, every color is easier to distinguish for people with deuteranopia, protanopia, and even tritanopia. These color choices are ideal for use in charts, wayfinding systems, and infographics, where color is key for interpreting information (**FIG 2.11**).

Designer Brian Suda has also experimented with color-blind-safe palettes. Not only does his palette translate well for a color-blind audience, but it also succeeds in grayscale, which can be helpful in some printing situations or on the monochromatic displays of various ereader devices (**FIG 2.12**).

Another useful tool I discovered has roots in a more traditional design industry—cartography. Professor Cynthia Brewer is a cartographer who developed an online tool called Color-Brewer, which provides color-palette advice originally intended for map design. One of the best things about this tool is that it also contains color-blind-friendly schemes that can be adapted for other applications (**FIG 2.13**).

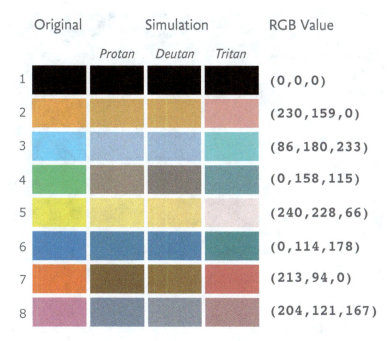

	Original	Simulation			RGB Value
		Protan	*Deutan*	*Tritan*	
1					(0,0,0)
2					(230,159,0)
3					(86,180,233)
4					(0,158,115)
5					(240,228,66)
6					(0,114,178)
7					(213,94,0)
8					(204,121,167)

FIG 2.11: Examples of colors more easily identified by color-blind people. (Adapted from CUDO's research.)

FIG 2.12: Brian Suda's set of color-blind-safe swatches.

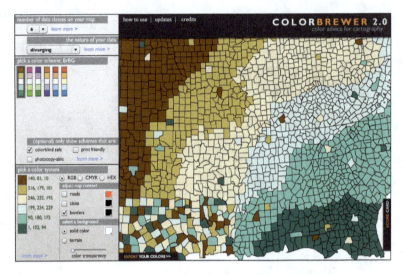

FIG 2.13: The ColorBrewer tool offers color advice for cartography.

Brewer explains that colors, including very similar colors, are much easier to differentiate when placed next to one another, much as they might appear in a map legend. It seems intuitive enough that comparing subtle color differences in close proximity is easier—think about how you'd overlap paint chips when picking out that perfect shade for your studio. A problem occurs, though, when the same colors are scattered in complex, random patterns: it becomes more difficult to locate which ones are unique. ColorBrewer demonstrates how a particular scheme will look when the color regions are close together, a little more spread out, or entirely random. If your scheme doesn't get a passing score, ColorBrewer will suggest reducing the number of data classes until you arrive at a clear and legible palette.

ColorBrewer lets you to choose color-blind-safe palettes in RGB, CMYK, and hex formats, and provides an ASE export function so you can load your generated palette straight into Photoshop or Illustrator.

We'll discuss additional tools to help you choose your palette in Chapter 3, after we learn about contrast compliance.

A word to the wise: choosing so-called "safe" and accessible colors may be met with opposition from higher-ups. In larger companies, such resistance may come from someone referred to in the industry as a "brand guardian". If forced to use on-brand color choices at the expense of legibility, try this counterargument: it's better to have a graph that looks slightly out of place but is easily deciphered than one that is on-brand but difficult to read. If customers can't make sense of something, they'll walk away.

CHECKING YOUR WORK

One of the first things I recommend to designers is integrating a color-blindness simulator into their workflow. Color-blindness simulators are indispensable tools for helping you assess whether you're on the right track from the start. Keep in mind, though, that not all color-blind people will see colors exactly as they appear in a simulator; simulators only mimic the vision of the most strongly affected people. Note that some differences in the simulated output may exist between different simulation applications—so be sure to remember the tips for choosing colors throughout your entire workflow and try not to rely on simulators as the only accessibility check in a project.

Mac OS X, Windows, and Linux users may want to try an application called Color Oracle. This indispensable tool displays common color-visual impairments as you use applications on your own screen. It's a full-screen filter that works throughout the operating system, independently of other software (FIG 2.14).

You can also proof for the two most common types of color blindness right in Photoshop or Illustrator (CS4 and later) as you're designing. This option is located under the View > Proof Setup menu in both applications (FIG 2.15).

Color simulators are excellent tools to have at your disposal—ideally, from the very beginning of a project—to help you make more informed color choices. Simulators alone, though, cannot guarantee your choices will be completely accessible. Next, we'll learn about color contrast ratios and compliance, which afford a more accurate way to evaluate your work.

FIG 2.14: Color Oracle works throughout the operating system and can simulate color blindness in any application.

FIG 2.15: Photoshop and Illustrator (CS4 and later) offer native color-blindness proofing.

COMPLIANCE AND TESTING

THE WEB CONTENT ACCESSIBILITY GUIDELINES (WCAG) 2.0 contain recommendations from the World Wide Web Consortium (W3C) for making the web more accessible to users with disabilities, including color blindness and other vision deficiencies.

There are three levels of conformance defined in WCAG 2.0, from lowest to highest: A, AA, and AAA. For text and images of text, AA is the minimum level that must be met.

AA compliance requires text and images of text to have a minimum color contrast ratio of 4.5:1. In other words, the lighter color in a pair must have four-and-a-half times as much luminance (an indicator of how bright a color will appear) as the darker color. This contrast ratio is calculated to include people with moderately low vision who don't need to rely on contrast-enhancing assistive technology, as well as people with color deficiencies. It's meant to compensate for the loss in contrast sensitivity often experienced by users with 20/40 vision, which is half of normal 20/20 vision.

Level AAA compliance requires a contrast ratio of 7:1, which provides compensation for users with 20/80 vision, or a quarter of normal 20/20 vision. People who have a degree of vision loss more than 20/80 generally require assistive technologies with contrast enhancement and magnification capabilities.

Text that acts as pure decoration, nonessential text that appears in part of a photograph, and images of company logos do not strictly need to adhere to these rules. Nonessential or decorative text is, by definition, not essential to understanding a page's content. Logos and wordmarks may contain textual elements that are essential to broadcasting the company's visual identity, but not to conveying important information. If necessary, the logo may be described by using an alt attribute for the benefit of a person using screen-reader software. To learn more, check out accessibility specialist Julie Grundy's blog post on Simply Accessible, where she goes into the best practices around describing alt attributes.

Text size plays a big role in determining how much contrast is required. Gray text with an RGB value of (150,150,150) on a pure white background passes the AA level of compliance, as long as it's used in headlines above 18 points. Gray text with an

AA | 18 pt Headline RGB(150,150,150)

X | This 10 pt body text with an RGB value of (150,150,150) does not pass AA compliance.

AAA | 18 pt Headline RGB(110,110,110)

AA | This 10 pt body text with an RGB value of (110,110,110) passes AA compliance at any level.

FIG 3.1: Text size also plays a role when calculating compliance ratios.

RGB value of (110,110,110) passes the AA level at any text size, and will be AAA compliant if used as a headline above 18 points (**FIG 3.1**). A font displayed at 14 points may have a different level of legibility compared to another font at 14 points due to the wide diversity of type styles, so keep this in mind, especially when using very thin weights.

Personally, I recommend that all body text be AAA compliant, with larger headlines and less important copy meeting AA compliance as a bare minimum. Keep in mind that these ratios refer to solid-colored text over solid-colored backgrounds, where a single color value can be measured. Overlaying text on a gradient, pattern, or photograph may require a higher contrast value or alternative placement, such as over a solid-colored strip, to provide sufficient legibility.

These compliance ratios are often what folks mean when they claim that achieving accessible design by "ticking off boxes" can only come at the cost of stifled creativity or restricted color choices. But that simply isn't true. Experimentation with a color-contrast checker proves that many compliance ratios are quite reasonable and easy to achieve—especially if you are aware of the rules from the beginning. It would be much more frustrating to try to shift poor color choices into something compliant later in the design process, after branding colors have already been chosen. If you fight your battles up front, you'll find you won't feel restricted at all.

If all this talk of numbers seems confusing, I promise there'll be no real math involved on your side. You can easily find out if your color pairs pass the test by using a color-contrast checker.

CONTRAST CHECKERS

One of my favorite tools is Lea Verou's Contrast Ratio (**FIG 3.2**). It gives you the option of entering a color code for a background and a color code for text, and it calculates the ratio for you.

Contrast Ratio supports color names, hex color codes, RGBA values, HSLA values, and even combinations of each. Supporting RGBA and HSLA values means that Verou's tool supports transparent colors, a handy feature. You can easily share the results of a check by copying and pasting the URL. Additionally, you can modify colors by changing the values in the URL string instead of using the page's input fields.

Another great tool that has the benefit of simultaneously showing whether a color combination passes both AA and AAA compliance levels is Jonathan Snook's Colour Contrast Check (**FIG 3.3**).

At the time of writing, Colour Contrast Check doesn't support HSL alpha values, but it does display the calculated brightness difference and color difference values, which might interest you if you want a little more information.

COLOR PICKERS

If you need help choosing accessible colors from the start, try Color Safe. This web-based tool helps designers experiment with and choose color combinations that are immediately contrast-compliant. Enter a background color as a starting point; then choose a standard font family, font size, font weight, and target WCAG compliance level. Color Safe will return a comprehensive list of suggestions that can be used as accessible text colors (**FIG 3.4**).

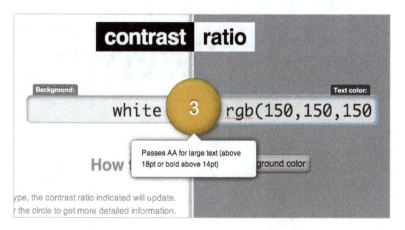

FIG 3.2: Lea Verou's Contrast Ratio checker.

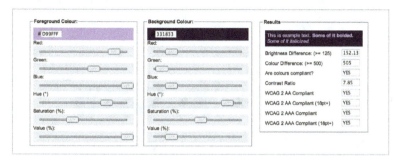

FIG 3.3: Jonathan Snook's Colour Contrast Check.

ADJUSTMENT TOOLS

When faced with color choices that fail the minimum contrast ratios, consider using something like Tanaguru Contrast Finder to help find appropriate alternatives (FIG 3.5). This incredibly useful tool takes a foreground and background color pair and then presents a range of compliant options comparable to the original colors. It's important to note that this tool works best when the colors are already close to being compliant but just need a little push—color pairs with drastically low contrast ratios may not return any suggestions at all (FIG 3.6).

FIG 3.4: Color Safe searches for compliant text colors based on an existing background color.

FIG 3.5: This color pair is not AA compliant.

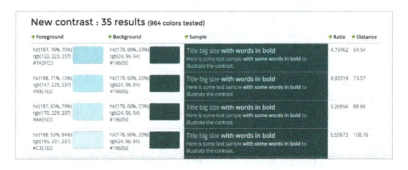

FIG 3.6: A selection of Tanaguru's suggested AA-compliant alternatives.

FIG 3.7: WAVE shows contrast errors by highlighting the relevant page elements.

TESTING TOOLS

If you'd like to test an existing website to see if it's up to par, check out a web-based service called WAVE. Although it evaluates for many different types of accessibility issues, it also features a contrast checker that pinpoints the exact location of any contrast hiccups on a given page. WAVE is also available as a Chrome Extension (**FIG 3.7**).

If Chrome is your preferred browser, try using Google's own Accessibility Developer Tools extension (**FIG 3.8**).

This tool allows you to inspect text elements and shows you the contrast ratio in a separate "Accessibility Properties" tab in the sidebar—very handy! You can run a full-page audit, too, for an extensive list of warnings (**FIG 3.9**).

Bear in mind, though, that it's important to take some of these warnings (or lack thereof) with a grain of salt. While audit tools like WAVE certainly can identify potential contrast errors in text, they only evaluate the issues they were programmed to evaluate; they can't predict exceptional circumstances. A site that passes such a test does not automatically mean it's accessible to a human being (**FIG 3.10**).

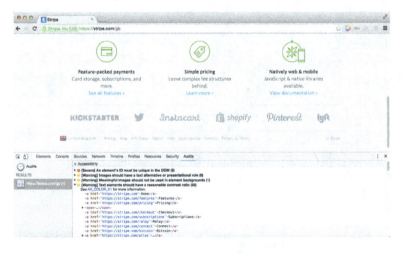

FIG 3.8: Accessibility audit screen in Chrome's Accessibility Developer Tools extension.

FIG 3.9: The accessibility properties inspector shows the insufficient contrast ratio warning for the gray text in the website's footer.

For example, because WAVE only checks for text contrast in relation to background colors, it doesn't notice that our red link in the introduction isn't underlined. For a person with protanopia or deuteranopia, this link will most likely blend into

FIG 3.10: WAVE can't pick up on all color contrast issues, such as the non-underlined red link in this introductory paragraph.

the surrounding paragraph text; yet it will not return a contrast error in the test results.

A similar issue occurs when using text over a photograph. Consider a screenshot of a website with legible white text placed over a darkened photograph (**FIG 3.11**). Now imagine what that would look like with images turned off in the browser settings (**FIG 3.12**). In this example, because the parent container is white, the text completely disappears unless it's highlighted with a cursor, as demonstrated for the screenshot. Turning off browser images is not just for folks with visual impairments. Expensive roaming costs may force travelers to save data wherever possible. Slow internet connections and older devices may struggle to load images at all. For these reasons, too, setting a contrast-compliant background color is crucial.

FIG 3.11: A section of the Apple iPad website with legible white text over a photograph.

FIG 3.12: The same text (highlighted) appears to be invisible if background images are turned off or are unable to load.

In 2012, Twitter rolled out site-wide profile header images that were overlaid on a dark-gray (#444) background color, which provided plenty of contrast to pass a contrast checker. However, because image colors weren't taken into account, if a Twitter user uploaded a photograph with poor contrast against the white text, it would not raise any alarms in a contrast check.

To take another example, running this Weather Network profile through WAVE returned warnings for various design elements on the page, but no contrast issue was flagged for the header, even though the photograph does not provide enough legibility for a person with a vision problem (FIG 3.13).

After I sampled an average color of the photograph and ran it through Lea Verou's checker, it showed that the contrast was

FIG 3.13: WAVE returns contrast errors for some page text, but not all.

a very low 2.3—well under the minimum 4.5 required for AA compliance.

In addition, absolutely positioned text elements that appear outside of their parent containers can return false positives. I discovered an example of this on an older iteration of the Flickr homepage. Running a test on the page showed me that the Forbes quote at the top didn't pass the test, even though it looked acceptable over the dark blue sky graphic (FIG 3.14).

When I inspected the page, I noticed that the whole banner was absolutely positioned. Because the parent container was white, the white-on-white text returned a false alarm (FIG 3.15).

Although these little quirks can certainly impact the results of a test, it's still worth running your work through a checker to catch any potential oversights.

We've covered a fair amount of ground so far. Now that we're equipped with knowledge of the fundamentals of color-accessible design, let's turn to how we might combine what we've learned to finesse the user experience.

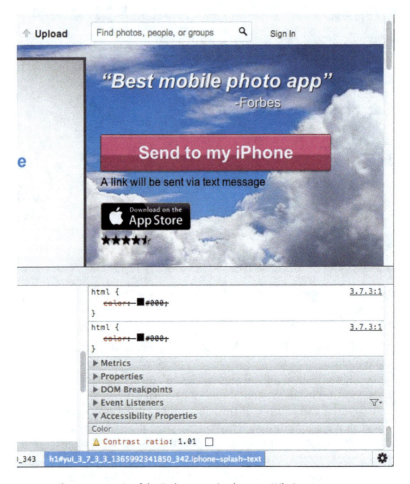

FIG 3.14: The contrast ratio of the Forbes quote is a low 1.01. Why?

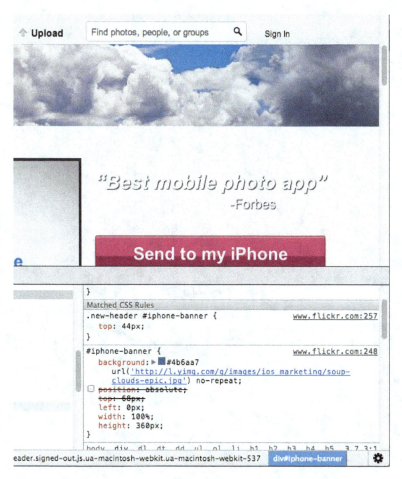

FIG 3.15: The parent container is absolutely positioned and the background is white.

4

TIPS AND TRICKS

ALTHOUGH CERTAIN COLOR COMBINATIONS should be avoided where possible, try not to spend too much time worrying about achieving a so-called "perfect" palette. You can use plenty of other tips and tricks in combination with your color choices to improve the user experience.

NAMING

What's in a name? A lot, if you're color-blind.

For people with good color vision, simple words like "red" or "green" can seem unnecessary or unimportant when labeling items, but they can relay essential information to a color-blind person who cannot otherwise tell the two apart.

Color names

If you design websites that sell products, especially clothing, you'll need to pay close attention to how those products are labeled. One of the most common complaints I hear from people affected by color blindness is that they find it difficult to purchase clothing and accessories; they frequently need to ask another person for a second opinion on what the color of the item might actually be. While it's often easier for someone with color blindness to shop online than in a physical store (where it may be embarrassing to have to ask a staff member or other customer to confirm a color), many accessibility issues can still crop up on ecommerce websites.

Imagine you're designing a website that sells T-shirts. If you only show a photo of the shirt, it may be impossible for someone with color blindness to tell what color the shirt really is. For clarification, be sure to reference the name of the color in the description of the product.

T-shirt designers United Pixelworkers (inactive at the time of writing) did a great job at following this rule on their original website (FIG 4.1). Their Indianapolis shirt, for example, was clearly described as having a "navy Indy car on a red American Apparel 100% cotton tee" with a "navy UP logo on the back."

FIG 4.1: United Pixelworkers provided helpful descriptions of their T-shirts' colors and patterns.

Another common problem occurs when a color filter has been added to a product search. Here's an example from L.L.Bean's website containing unlabeled color swatches, and how they might look to someone with deuteranopia (**FIG 4.2**).

The color-search filter from an earlier version of the H&M website, which uses names instead, is slightly better, but this method can create unnecessary problems too (**FIG 4.3**).

The concept of completely stripping color from a design as a means of making things "easier" to comprehend for all audiences has been explored in other ways. Nathalie Dubé, a Canadian designer, experimented with this topic in a student project where she redesigned colored pencils to be all white, with a label printed on each stating the color name in French (**FIG 4.4**). Although this might make sense in theory, removing the color coating from each pencil also effaced a visual cue that could have made it easier to find the pencils at a glance.

It's important to remember that most so-called color-blind people can still see some color, and are capable of narrowing down such choices based on their own abilities. A color-blind person may not know which exact pencil is red, but they may know which pencils are *not* red, and therefore can eliminate many choices up front if a colored label exists. They can then

Good color vision   Deuteranopia

FIG 4.2: The color-search filter on L.L.Bean's website is no help at all to color-blind visitors.

FIG 4.3: On an earlier version of its site, H&M provided color names for its search filter, but matching swatches would have improved matters even further.

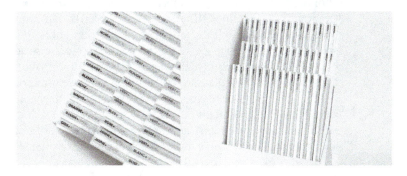

FIG 4.4: Nathalie Dubé's project erases color entirely, making pencil selection more difficult for everyone.

continue reading the labels to find the red in question. Removing color completely not only forces color-blind people to read every single label before making a choice, but forces everyone else to do the same.

The best solution is to use a combination of colors *and* names. Not only will that benefit people with good color vision, allowing them to scan swatches quickly, but it will also give color-blind users a reference and a name to work with. The American eyewear company Warby Parker has a robust search filter on its website, with a very effective combination of color swatches and names (FIG 4.5). The ability to increase the size of the swatch sample also helps reduce confusion.

"Creative" names

The color spectrum is continuous, and it is language that cuts it up. It is neither in nature nor in our eye that orange ceases to be orange and becomes red, nor in the speaking subjects who, faced with such a sample of color, decide its name. It is in the language that gave them the choice of words. If the English language had not placed orange between yellow and red, how are we to know that the perception of it would not have been different?

—THIERRY DE DUVE, Pictorial Nominalism: On Marcel Duchamp's Passage from Painting to the Readymade

As helpful as naming can be for describing the color of clothing or products, try not to get too fancy with your word choices. "Creative" color names, like the ones you might find on swatches of paint samples, can be just as confusing as not using any color name at all (FIG 4.6). Using a word like "grape" instead of "purple" doesn't really give the viewer any useful information about what the actual hue is. Is grape supposed to be purple, or could it refer to red or even green grapes? What about the name "smoke"? While you might intend for it to mean gray, smoke can also appear to be white, black, or brown, and colored smoke exists too. Stick with hue names as much as possible—there's

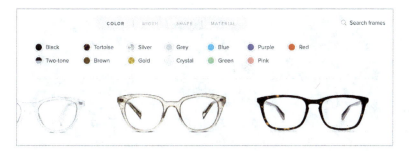

FIG 4.5: Warby Parker provides both color names and swatches—the most effective solution.

FIG 4.6: The color combinations of these men's sweaters are described on the Superdry website as Woodland/Sky, Iced Coffee/Apple, and Ashes/Coral, respectively.

a greater chance that the viewer will understand that a red shirt is red rather than brick, and it won't force them to ask another person for clarification.

This makes a huge case for why we always need to keep color-blind users in mind (**FIG 4.7**). How many potential customers might you lose because of a single design decision? Chances are, quite a few—especially if you're selling menswear!

FIG 4.7: How a person with tritanopia might view these sweaters. The color names carry little meaning.

IMAGES AND TEXT

Overlaying text on an image is an extremely common design technique that needs more consideration. Pay attention to the areas of an image where the text contrast and image contrast could become illegible to a person with vision problems (**FIG 4.8**). When in doubt, consider adding a solid background with the sufficient contrast necessary to keep the text visible no matter what kind of image is placed underneath (**FIG 4.9**). Alternatively, try making the image subtler by masking it with a darker color for lighter text, or a lighter color for darker text (**FIG 4.10**).

DATA AND INFOGRAPHICS

Designing accessible maps and infographics can be quite a challenge, especially since color is often chosen as the sole indicator of different data regions (**FIG 4.11**).

Don't rely on color-coding alone. Use a combination of color and texture or pattern, along with precise labels, and reflect this in the key or legend. That way, readers will always have two pieces of information to work with (**FIG 4.12**).

The patterns you choose can matter too. As a rule of thumb, a lighter shade of a background color should contain a subtler pattern design, such as a sparse dot or thin vertical line. A darker

FIG 4.8: In some areas of this photo, the text is illegible against the background.

FIG 4.9: Experimenting with placing text on a solid block or bar yields better results.

FIG 4.10: Stylizing images can help make text stand out.

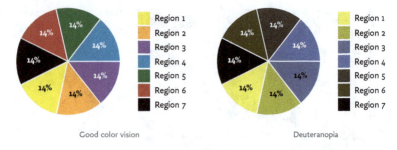

		Good color vision				Deuteranopia

FIG 4.11: This chart contains colors that may cause confusion.

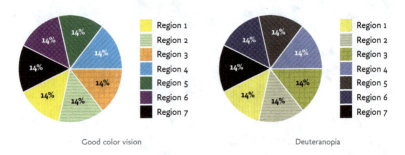

FIG 4.12: This chart contains improved color choices overall and adds a pattern to each type of data. The patterns are reflected in the key for improved legibility.

background color can contain a more complex pattern design, such as a square or diamond grid (FIG 4.13). When a complex pattern is placed over a lighter color, it can trick the eye into appearing darker than it really is. In general, consider making the pattern design darker in color than the background color it sits on, since a darker pattern may be easier to distinguish than a lighter one (FIG 4.14).

Line graphs can be difficult to read if they contain intersecting paths (FIG 4.15).

Try varying the thickness of each line, giving each a different style, and adding direct labels (FIG 4.16).

Introducing color to the backgrounds of infographics can also create confusion; avoid doing so if it negatively impacts legibility. Placing each chart on a solid white background can help keep the data as clear as possible.

FIG 4.13: Complex patterns can be difficult for people with low vision to distinguish.

FIG 4.14: Dark, subtle patterns placed over a lighter background color can be more effective.

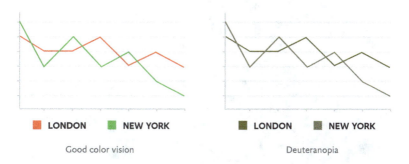

FIG 4.15: This graph's intersecting lines are difficult for people with deuteranopia to distinguish.

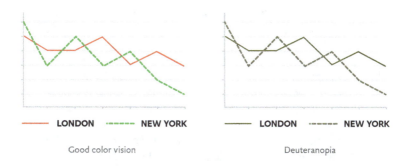

FIG 4.16: This line graph is improved by adding a second line style for redundancy.

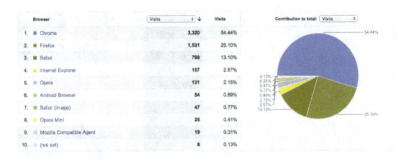

	Browser	Visits ⬍ ↓	Visits		Contribution to total:	Visits ⬍
1.	■ Chrome	3,320	54.44%			54.44%
2.	■ Firefox	1,531	25.10%			
3.	■ Safari	799	13.10%			
4.	■ Internet Explorer	157	2.57%			
5.	■ Opera	131	2.15%			
6.	■ Android Browser	54	0.89%			
7.	■ Safari (in-app)	47	0.77%			
8.	■ Opera Mini	25	0.41%			25.10%
9.	■ Mozilla Compatible Agent	19	0.31%			
10.	■ (not set)	8	0.13%			

FIG 4.17: This simulated view of Google Analytics shows how labels pointing to each data region make the information easier to parse.

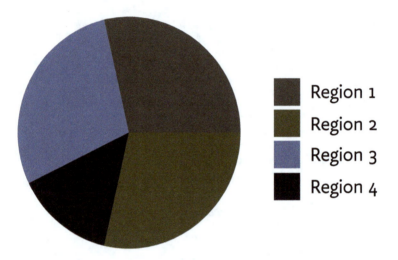

FIG 4.18: This simulated view shows unlabeled data regions, which can be confusing.

A pie-chart view for browser statistics on Google Analytics is color-coded with each slice directly labeled; it works well, even if many of the colors appear to be similar (**FIG 4.17**).

However, an example of an unlabeled chart demonstrates that even a simple chart with just three data regions can become confusing when colors look nearly identical (**FIG 4.18**).

MAPS AND WAYFINDING SYSTEMS

The map of the London Underground is an iconic image not just in London, but around the world (**FIG 4.19**). Unfortunately, for a person with a vision problem, it contains some colors that appear indistinguishable from one another (**FIG 4.20**).

This is true not only for the London Underground, but also for any other wayfinding system that relies on color-coding as the only key in a legend.

Printable versions of the map exist online in black and white, using distinguishable patterns and shades of black and gray, but it's interesting to note that the actual wayfinding signage in place in the subway system is colored; the grayscale patterns can't be found in use. Still, this map is a helpful option for deciphering routes on paper (**FIG 4.21**).

FIG 4.19: The map of the London Underground contains colors that can pose problems for a person with a color-vision deficiency.

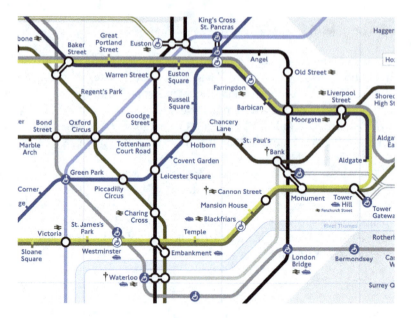

FIG 4.20: How a person with protanopia might view the London subway map.

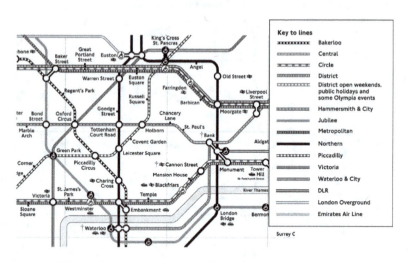

FIG 4.21: A black-and-white version of the London Underground map.

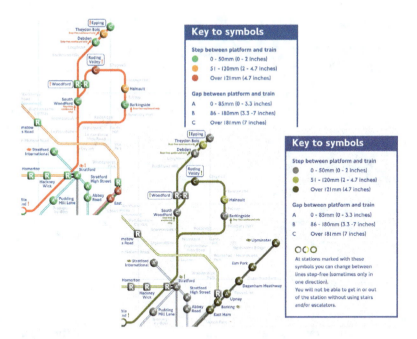

FIG 4.22: The step-free map as it might look to a person with deuteranopia.

If you're someone who has a physical disability as well as a vision problem, the step-free guide map has some very poor color-coding for step height between platforms and trains, and doesn't clearly indicate which stations have step-free line changes (**FIG 4.22**).

Paul Wynne designed a map to be used by both color-blind and non-color-blind people. He added a simple pattern to each line and reflected that in the key, and he attached color names to each line in case he received verbal directions from another person. He explains that now, if someone tells him to take the brown line and change to the red line, he can follow along with his version of the map (**FIG 4.23**).

By contrast, the Tokyo Metro map is designed to be accessible from the start. Although it too has different colors for different subway lines, each line is also given a letter of the English alphabet, and every station on that line is labeled with a

Key to lines and symbols

Bakerloo (Brown)		Metropolitan (Magenta)	
Central (Red)		Northern (Black)	
Circle (Yellow)		Piccadilly (Dark Blue)	
District (Green)		Victoria (Light Blue)	
East London (Maintenance -Check For Details)		Waterloo & City (Turquoise)	
Hammersmith & City (Pink)		Docklands Light Railway	
Jubilee (Grey)		National Rail	

FIG 4.23: Paul Wynne's custom color-accessible London Underground map.

numeral. Takebashi station, also known as T-08, can therefore be intuitively understood as the eighth stop on the Tozai line. Not only does this make it easier for people with color blindness to understand, but it also helps non-Japanese speakers find stations based on letters and numerals rather than on unfamiliar words. Numerals also help riders understand the direction of the train when riding, as well as the number of stops left until their destination—an added benefit to travelers with low vision who must rely on announcements. The system's physical signage is consistent throughout the network, making wayfinding easier for everyone (**FIG 4.24**).

Some color-blind people have no difficulty navigating environments that depend on color-coding; others can decipher them after careful study. In a subway system, taking a little extra time to work out a map may not pose much of a problem, but remember to consider environments like hospitals and healthcare centers, where time can literally be a matter of life and death.

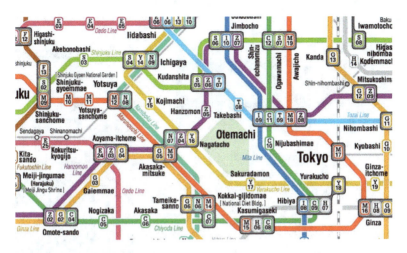

FIG 4.24: Every station on the Tokyo Metro subway is labeled with a color, letter, and numeral.

LINKS

One of the most common issues on the web occurs when, for aesthetic reasons, designers and developers remove the default text-decoration: underline CSS property on hyperlinks. Although many links are obvious based on context and location on the page (think navigation menus), links that appear within a paragraph of text can blend in if they lack another cue to make them stand out.

We ran into this problem when designing the website for the W3C's Responsive Image Community Group.

The red link contained in the black paragraph text was completely invisible. Although we had an underline on hover, it wasn't enough—we can't expect users to hover over sections of text with the hope that a link will come into view. Besides, hover states aren't perceptible on mobile devices (**FIG 4.25**).

If you don't want to underline the link, consider increasing its font weight or adding other visual cues, like framing or blocked background colors. Remember to be consistent—when using underlines as a link style, try to refrain from using underlines elsewhere in the design for other functions such as empha-

RES ONSIVE IMAGES C **MMUNITY G** UP

W e a group of de elopers worl ng
to ards a markup- ased mean f
de ering alternate image sou es
based c n device cap bilities to prevent
wasted ban width and opti nize display
for both scree and print.

FIG 4.25: The link contained in this paragraph practically disappears in this protanopia-type color blindness simulation.

sis, since that could cause issues for folks with cognitive disabilities too. If all else fails, and you are for whatever reason required to keep links undecorated and differentiated purely by color, be sure to make the contrast between the link and surrounding text at least 3:1. An example of this would be standard #000000 black paragraph text, with a teal link color of #007777 that has a contrast ratio of 3.9:1; the #007777 remains legible on a white page background with a contrast ratio of 5.4:1.

In addition, for readers who rely on keyboard navigation to find their way around a website, remember to supply a different visual enhancement not only on mouseover, but also on focus states. Consider adding an outline or different background color to links to differentiate them when highlighted (**FIG 4.26**).

FIG 4.26: The website for An Event Apart adds yellow backgrounds to indicate focused links for visitors using keyboard navigation.

FORMS

Visual cues are important in form design too. Avoid labeling required fields with colored text only (**FIG 4.27**). It's safer to indicate required fields with supporting text in the label, or with a symbol cue like an asterisk, which is color-independent (**FIG 4.28**).

WCAG notes that asterisks may not be successfully parsed by all screen readers, and that they may be difficult for users with low vision to see, since they're often rendered in a smaller size than the default text. Furthermore, by introducing an extra layer of abstraction, asterisks may also pose difficulties for people with cognitive disabilities. A safer solution would be simply to label the field with direct instructions. If most fields are required but just a few are optional, mark the optional fields as "optional". If most fields are optional but just a few are required, mark the required fields as "required". This cuts down on the visual noise of a large number of labels and presents clearer instructions on how to complete the form.

Pay special attention to validation, too. If a form field is not filled out correctly, avoid highlighting the error with color alone; a red border may not be visible at all to some color-blind people and is meaningless. If you use a colored border, be sure to reinforce it with a clear error message.

Okay, enough theory. It's time to put everything we've learned into practice as we tackle color accessibility in our projects.

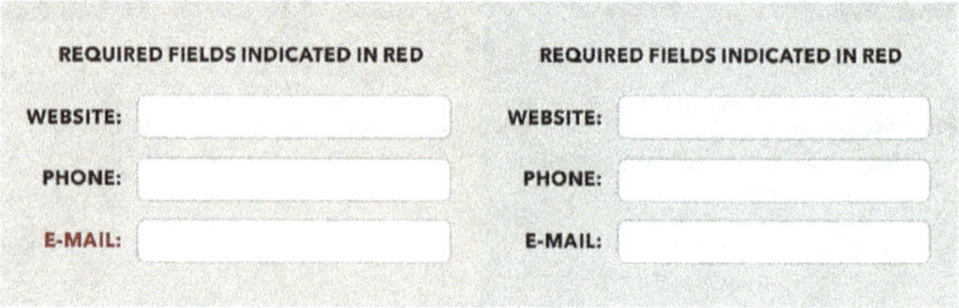

FIG 4.27: Avoid designing forms with color as the only indicator of a required field.

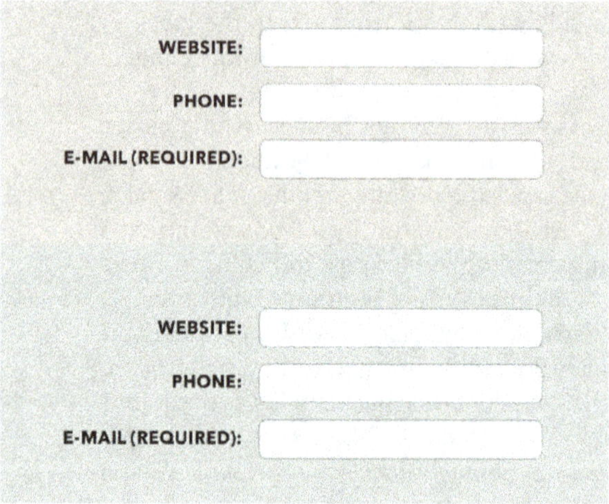

FIG 4.28: This form offers a better solution; its labels can be parsed by a screen reader.

IMPLEMENTATION

LEARNING THE VARIOUS TIPS AND TRICKS for making a website color-accessible may seem straightforward until the time comes to weave them into your existing workflow. Although project management approaches vary for every designer, developer, and team, it may be helpful to read a case study on how we tackled the website redesign for Simply Accessible.

Founded by Derek Featherstone, Simply Accessible is a group of accessibility specialists whose goal is to change the perception of accessibility on the web. A tired, outdated website lying fallow due to busy client projects provided the perfect opportunity for a total overhaul to show the world what the company really stood for: accessible design that is always inclusive but never boring.

CREATE A COLOR GAME PLAN

During the early stages of redesign research, I like to do a deep audit of the existing color usage across the entire brand. Gathering every instance of color and organizing it into a document can, at a glance, help you understand what should be dropped, added, or revamped. Almost certainly, it will show you just how many versions of a single color can creep its way into the code, especially in projects worked on by multiple people.

Some branding evolutions will keep an existing logo and introduce fresh colors (think Coca-Cola and its updated blacks, greens, and silvers for new bottles); others will preserve their iconic colors but usher in new logo styles (think Pepsi and its traditional red, white, and blue).

For Simply Accessible, both of these options proved difficult. There was no established logo to carry into the new design, and to call the name a "wordmark" was a stretch. The brand's typeface, Helvetica, lacked character by definition. The only feature left to work with was color. And even that was a challenge—the oranges looked murky and brown, and the blues looked far too corporate and "safe" for a company like Simply Accessible (FIG 5.1).

With our evaluation complete, we dug in deep and played around with some ideas to inject new life into our palette.

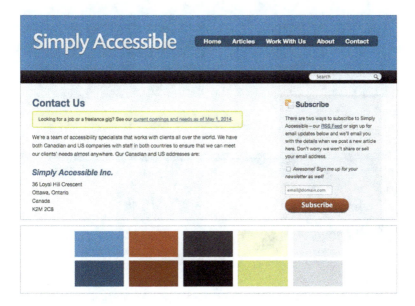

FIG 5.1: The original Simply Accessible website.

Develop color concepts

After much experimentation, we settled on a simple, two-color palette of blue and orange—a warm-cool contrast color scheme. We added swatches for call-to-action messaging in green, error messaging in red, and body copy and form fields in black and gray. Shades and tints of blue and orange were added to illustrations and other design elements for extra detail and interest (**FIG 5.2**).

If circumstances allow it, consider introducing new color choices to an internal, private project before jumping in and going public. Even applying fresh colors to something as simple as a report or presentation can allow plenty of time to get a feel for the design and work out any uncertainties. At Simply Accessible, we tested our initial palette on an internal report (**FIG 5.3**).

It's important to be open to changes in your palette; it may need to evolve throughout the design process. One of the biggest mistakes you can make at this stage is telling your client

FIG 5.2: Our first stab at a new palette.

FIG 5.3: Putting the test palette through its paces with an internal report.

that any given palette design is final—it's better to explain that it's actually a flexible concept that can adapt and grow. If you need to tweak the color of a button later because of legibility issues, the last thing you want is your client pushing back because it's different from what you promised.

As it happened, we did tweak the colors after the test run, and we even adjusted the new logo—what looked great printed on paper looked a little too light on device screens.

Consider how colors might be used

If you haven't had the opportunity to test your palette in advance, don't worry. As long as you have some well-considered options, you'll be prepared to think about the various ways that color might be used on your site or app.

Unless you're designing a small, static, one-off project that will never grow or evolve, it's unlikely you'll know every design element required for launch date, or what could potentially

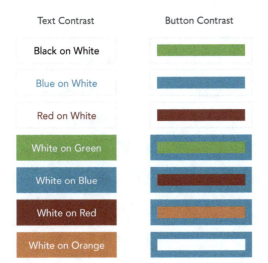

Text Contrast	Button Contrast
Black on White	
Blue on White	
Red on White	
White on Green	
White on Blue	
White on Red	
White on Orange	

FIG 5.4: A variety of potential combinations of text color and background color, and button color and background color.

be introduced to the site down the road. There are, of course, plenty of good places to start.

For Simply Accessible, I mocked up some examples in Illustrator to get a handle on the elements where contrast and legibility matter the most: text and background colors (**FIG 5.4**). While it's less crucial to consider the contrast of decorative elements that don't convey essential information, it's still important for a reader to be able to discern elements like button shapes, empty form fields, and focus states.

Run initial tests

Once these elements were laid out, I manually plugged the HTML color code of each foreground and background color into Lea Verou's Contrast Checker. I added the results from each color pair test to my document so we could see at a glance which colors needed adjustment and which colors wouldn't work at all (**FIG 5.5**).

As you can see, this test exposed a few problems. To meet the minimum AA compliance, we needed to slightly darken the green, blue, and orange background colors for text—an easy

Text Contrast

Black on White
Ratio: 21.00
AA Large: Pass   AAA Large: Pass
AA Small: Pass   AAA Small: Pass

Blue on White
Ratio: 4.7
AA Large: Pass   AAA Large: Pass
AA Small: Pass   AAA Small: Pass

Red on White
Ratio: 8.23
AA Large: Pass   AAA Large: Pass
AA Small: Pass   AAA Small: Pass

White on Green
Ratio: 3.26
AA Large: Pass   AAA Large: *Fail*
AA Small: *Fail*   AAA Small: *Fail*

White on Blue
Ratio: 4.66
AA Large: Pass   AAA Large: Pass
AA Small: Pass   AAA Small: *Fail*

White on Red
Ratio: 8.23
AA Large: Pass   AAA Large: Pass
AA Small: Pass   AAA Small: Pass

White on Orange
Ratio: 3.36
AA Large: Pass   AAA Large: *Fail*
AA Small: *Fail*   AAA Small: *Fail*

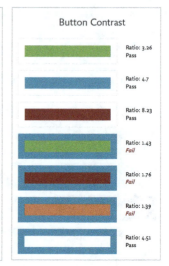

Button Contrast

Ratio: 3.26
Pass

Ratio: 4.7
Pass

Ratio: 8.23
Pass

Ratio: 1.43
Fail

Ratio: 1.76
Fail

Ratio: 1.39
Fail

Ratio: 4.51
Pass

FIG 5.5: This diagram revealed that three text- and background-color combinations had contrast-ratio issues.

FIG 5.6: This diagram showed that three button and background-color combinations had contrast-ratio issues.

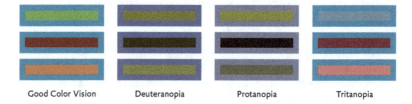

Good Color Vision   Deuteranopia   Protanopia   Tritanopia

FIG 5.7: How our proposed color pairs might look to people with three types of color blindness.

fix. A more complicated glitch emerged with the button colors. Although I had envisioned some buttons appearing over a blue background, the contrast ratios ended up being well under 3:1 (**FIG 5.6**). Although there isn't a guide in WCAG for contrast requirements of two non-text elements, the *International Organization for Standardization* (ISO) and *American National Standards Institute* (ANSI) standard for visible contrast is 3:1, which is what we decided to aim for.

We also checked our color combinations in Color Oracle, which confirmed that colored buttons over blue backgrounds simply wouldn't work. The contrast was much too low, especially for the more common deuteranopia- and protanopia-type deficiencies (FIG 5.7).

Make adjustments if necessary

We adjusted our colors using the Tanaguru Contrast Finder to achieve accessible versions of our green, blue, and orange background-text colors. We also opted to change all buttons to white when they were used over dark backgrounds; this increased contrast and made the button design across the site more consistent. It also helped us avoid introducing a lot of unnecessary color variants, which could cause potential confusion when navigating the site.

You'll probably find that putting more effort into achieving compliant contrast ratios at this stage will make the rest of implementation and testing much easier. When you've got your ratios looking good, you can move on to implementation.

IMPLEMENT THE PALETTE IN A STYLE GUIDE AND PROTOTYPE

Once I was happy with my contrast checks, I created a basic style guide and added all the color values from my color exploration files (FIG 5.8), introduced more tints and shades for use in detail work and illustrations, and added patterned backgrounds. I created examples of every panel style we intended to use on the site, with sample text, links, and buttons—all with working hover states and focus states (FIG 5.9). Adding color to a working style guide not only makes things easier for the developers, but it also facilitates further contrast checks and testing in an actual broWSER.

White #FFFFFF Light Blue #EEF8F9 Blue #008AB4 Dark Blue #0C4C6F

Light Orange #FCEDE3 Orange #C9472D Red #AF2D2D Dark Red #991F1F

Light Grey #DDD Grey #BBB Dark Grey #333 Black #000

FIG 5.8: Adding basic color swatches to a style guide.

FIG 5.9: A variety of panels with text, button, and background-color combinations in a working style guide.

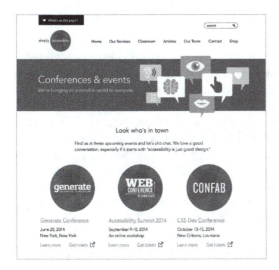

FIG 5.10: Designing in grayscale may help you focus on contrast between important elements before introducing color.

WORKING IN GRAYSCALE

Gray has no agenda... Gray has the ability, that no other color has, to make the invisible visible.
—**ROMA TEARNE**, Mosquito

In the early stages of designing actual page wireframes or layouts, it can be helpful to ignore your newly chosen color palette and work in grayscale instead. If you can strike the right balance and create a legible, attractive design here, chances are it will work when you introduce your color choices, and will have a better chance of retaining the contrast necessary for the needs of a wider audience (**FIG 5.10**).

Many of the initial concepts for the Simply Accessible website were designed this way, in grayscale, even though we already had a palette in mind. It allowed us to focus on the content that mattered most and let us push out faster page layouts, rather than worrying too much about where each particular color should go.

PREFLIGHT CHECK

Before launch day, it's a good idea to do a final check for color accessibility issues to ensure that nothing has been lost in translation from the intended design to the actual code, especially when working with a large team. Fortunately, at this stage, unless you've introduced massive changes to the design in the prototype, it should be fairly easy to fix any issues that arise, especially if you've stayed on top of updating any revisions in the style guide. If it isn't feasible at this point in time to check every single page, particularly on a large website, select a representative sample of various types of pages to evaluate instead.

WAVE is great to use here because it works in any browser. However, if your site doesn't have a public link, it's better to use the built-in Chrome Accessibility Tools (FIG 5.11).

THE HUMAN TOUCH

Ultimately, no amount of careful planning or evaluation reports can compare to the feedback received from real humans with abilities and disabilities of all kinds. If you're unsure of how something may be viewed by people with a color-vision deficiency, reach out and ask for their opinions and experiences. Involve them in the early stages of design and development—not just as an afterthought. At the same time, remember not to jump to conclusions based on a single person's advice, since disabilities cannot be generalized. Combining user feedback with evaluation tools and best practices is your safest bet.

Although Simply Accessible's final palette diverged from our initial ideas, we were pleased that it wasn't merely compliant, but also showed the company's true personality, with plenty of room to expand and evolve (FIG 5.12).

Keeping these pointers in mind should help you gain a better understanding of how to weave color accessibility into a project from the start. Next, we'll discuss how to tackle less-than-ideal implementations of color accessibility—when it arrives as an afterthought, fix, or add-on feature. And trust me, it will. Life is messy that way.

FIG 5.11: Chrome's Accessibility Tools audit feature shows no immediate issues with color contrast in our prototype.

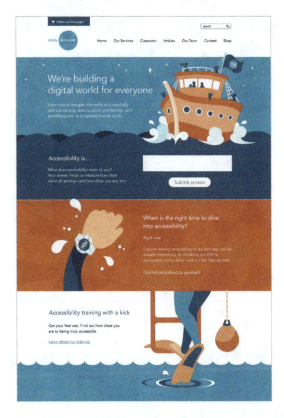

FIG 5.12: The redesigned Simply Accessible website.

PROVIDING
ALTERNATIVES

"EASIER SAID THAN DONE!" That's what some of you may be thinking about the actual implementation of color-accessible design. In the real world, circumstances sometimes hinder designers or developers from influencing the opinions of higher-ups, like skeptical bosses or clients who refuse to back down from poor design decisions. On top of that, you may already have a product with major accessibility issues in need of fixing. If that's the case, consider providing alternative styles or allowing users to edit their own colors.

WEBSITES AND APPS

The iChat application for macOS is no longer available, but it remains a good example of such features (FIG 6.1). Although, by default, it used colored bubbles to indicate a user's status (available for chat, away or idle, or busy), the preferences included a Use Shapes to Indicate Status option, which changed the standard circles to green circles, yellow triangles, and red squares, respectively (FIG 6.2).

If the style of your app, website, or game is low-contrast by default, consider adding a style switcher either as a setting or as a button in a visible location. Check out the example on Belgian designer Veerle Pieter's blog. She drops the colored backgrounds, inverts the text color, and changes link colors—simply by loading a new style sheet (FIG 6.3).

Some operating systems, like Windows, have built-in high-contrast modes that are popular among readers with low vision. Unfortunately, because of limitations in the way such modes handle images, some website icons and images don't translate well and may disappear completely when a high-contrast mode is enabled.

If SVG icons or images are essential to your website's design, consider using Boston-based developer Eric Bailey's method for modifying them through CSS media queries, using a lesser-known feature that allows you to directly target Windows' High Contrast Mode:

FIG 6.1: The default status bubbles of the iChat application were not color-blind-friendly.

FIG 6.2: iChat contained an alternative set of color-blind-friendly icons consisting of shapes in addition to colors.

Normal view

High contrast

FIG 6.3: Adding a high-contrast style sheet to your website can help many readers.

FIG 6.4: Example of two side-by-side icons with High Contrast Mode enabled. One is poor; the other has been tweaked using media queries.

Default High Contrast view   Corrected using media queries

```
/* Targets displays using any of Windows' High
   Contrast Mode themes: */
@media screen and (-ms-high-contrast: active) { }
/* Targets displays using Windows' High Contrast
   Black theme: */
@media screen and (-ms-high-contrast: white-on-
   black) { }
/* Targets displays using Windows' High Contrast
   White theme: */
@media screen and (-ms-high-contrast: black-on-
   white) { }
```

Using this code, a problematic icon can be targeted and given higher-contrast colors that will retain their contrast when High Contrast Mode is active (**FIG 6.4**).

GAME DESIGN

Let's talk more specifically about game design. At the time of writing, Niantic's Pokémon GO, an augmented-reality game that was awarded five Guinness World Records in August 2016 and became an overnight social media phenomenon, contained problematic gameplay elements for people with color-vision deficiency. PokéStops, a feature where players must physically visit locations to restock on game items, relied only on color to show players if the stop had already been visited (FIG 6.5). This poses obvious problems for someone with red-green color blindness (FIG 6.6).

Niantic isn't the only developer guilty of poor color accessibility; it's a major issue in video game design. I asked a group of color-blind people which medium or form of entertainment was the most difficult to read or use, and multiple people noted that video games needed the most improvement. One man argued that game developers don't seem to pay much attention to color at all, even when it's an essential part of gameplay. It's easy to understand why he might feel this way: game developers often focus on flashy graphics designed to impress, but leave humbler interface design elements as an afterthought. This results in a poor user experience, even for a person with good vision. Combine that with the fact that many games rely on the use of color as an essential game mechanism, and you end up with some games being completely unplayable for a significant part of the population.

Color-blind gamers have been increasingly vocal online, urging developers to release updates to enhance games that weren't designed with color-vision deficiencies in mind. A 2011 BBC article interviewed Kathryn Albany-Ward, founder of the UK group Color Blind Awareness, who suggested that game developers place warnings on the game packaging or download page if good color vision is a requirement for enjoyable gameplay. "It's like a 'contains traces of nuts' label," she explained, "so at least you know you're not wasting your money."

Fortunately, some companies are starting to listen to this feedback. Every release in Activision's popular *Call of Duty* series since *Modern Warfare 3* allows players to change team

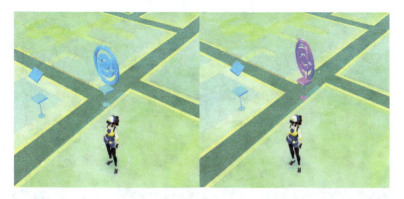

FIG 6.5: How unvisited and visited PokéStops look to a person with normal color vision.

FIG 6.6: Unvisited and visited PokéStops can appear the same for a person with red-green color blindness.

indicators from a confusing red-and-green pair to a more legible light-blue-and-orange pair. Blizzard's huge title *World of Warcraft* now includes three sets of filters to assist people with all three forms of color blindness, and can be personalized with a "strength" slider depending on how severe one's condition is (FIG 6.7).

The developers of the game *Faster Than Light* created an alternate mode for color blindness and asked for public feedback to make sure it passed the test. And for the most part it

FIG 6.7: World of Warcraft games include customizable color-blind filters to improve the gaming experience.

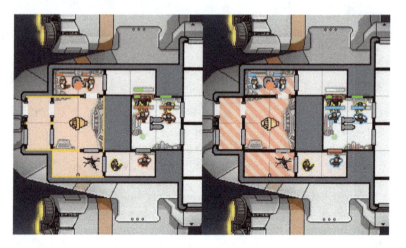

FIG 6.8: Normal game mode and color-blind game mode in *Faster Than Light*.

FIG 6.9: AudioSurf allows gamers to choose their own colors.

did—though adding stripes to the red zones and changing outlines to blue instead of green made all the difference (FIG 6.8).

The game AudioSurf from indie developer Dylan Fitterer uses players' own music to create the puzzles in each level. Players gain points by clustering blocks of the same color on the highway, and the settings include an option for people to choose their own colors, whether out of personal preference or out of necessity due to visual impairment (FIG 6.9).

Many game developers are heading in the right direction and understand the importance of color accessibility; others, alas, still have a long way to go. In the 2011 BBC article I mentioned earlier about color blindness in gaming, industry giants Nintendo told the BBC that while its developers do try to make their games as accessible as possible, it was "not possible to cater to the needs of all the players 100% of the time." Although there may be some truth in that statement—designing interfaces to support those with color deficiencies will still leave out many people who are completely blind—it sounds quite defensive and dismissive. In my opinion, that's the wrong attitude to take.

CONCLUSION

IN DISCUSSIONS AROUND ACCESSIBILITY, you may hear people ask "how much work" is required or "how many features" are necessary to make a website accessible, as if that can be quantified. Let's think more positively. Let's ask: "How can I make this as inclusive as possible?" And: "How can I make this more accessible than before?"

Accessibility expert Derek Featherstone explains that many people believe doing "something" is better than doing nothing at all, even if that "something" means subpar accessibility with less than optimal access. He states that we all need to aim for the stars, set a high standard, and keep pushing ourselves to do more to include as many people as we can. I couldn't agree with him more.

Maybe we should all take a cue from developer Mat Marquis, who, in a 2012 talk on responsible design, declared:

> When I build a website, my goal is to build a website for anyone who cares to use it. Maybe I don't always get everything 100% right, but I'm going to keep trying. And when someone asks me why I couldn't make something work? "I'm trying" is a damn sight better answer than "because I didn't have to."

Like elegant typography, engaging content, and efficient code, color is yet another powerful tool at our disposal for crafting enjoyable user experiences on the web. I hope these color accessibility tips will become an important part of every responsible designer's workflow as we strive to make the web accessible to all. Let's not leave anyone behind.

ACKNOWLEDGMENTS

SPECIAL THANKS GO TO Emma and Mark Boulton and the original Five Simple Steps team for publishing my first book on color accessibility before they closed their doors. I'm so grateful to be able to continue writing about this important topic for A Book Apart.

To my team—Katel LeDû, Caren Litherland, Tina Lee, and Jason Santa Maria, you have been an absolute pleasure to work with. Thank you, Jeffrey Zeldman, for giving me this wonderful opportunity.

Thank you, Jon Hicks, for being my technical editor. Your input as a colorblind designer has been invaluable. Thank you, Dr. Meghann Mears, for helping me explain the more scientific side of things and for your support as a friend.

Thank you to Derek Featherstone and the whole Simply Accessible team for all the incredible work that you do to make the digital world a better, more inclusive place for everyone.

And, of course, thank you Simon (and Bearface) for your love and support.

RESOURCES

Articles

- "Are colour blind gamers left out?" by Dave Lee for *BBC News*
- "New Outlook on Colorblindness" by Melinda Beck for the *Wall Street Journal*
- "Say What You See: How does colour-blindness affect the property sector?" (PDF) by Noella Pio Kivlehan for *Estates Gazette*

Research

- "Cognitive Disabilities" by WebAIM
- We Are Colorblind
- Colblindor
- Colour Blind Awareness
- "Colour Vision: Almost Reason Enough for Having Eyes" (PDF) by Jay Neitz, Joseph Carroll, and Maureen Neitz

Tools

- Web Content Accessibility Guidelines 2.0
- Contrast ratio by Lea Verou
- Colour contrast check by Jonathan Snook
- Color Oracle by Bernhard Jenny
- Tanaguru Contrast Finder
- WAVE Web Accessibility Evaluation Tool
- "Color Design for the Color Vision Impaired—Mapping: Methods & Tips"(PDF) by Bernhard Jenny and Nathaniel Vaughn Kelso
- "Accessible Color Swatches" by Brian Suda
- Colblindor compilation of tests
- Waggoner Computerized Color Vision Test
- EnChroma online test
- DanKam—an augmented-reality application for color-blind users

REFERENCES

Shortened URLs are numbered sequentially; the related long URLs are listed below for reference.

Introduction

00-01 https://en.wikipedia.org/wiki/The_dress

Chapter 1

01-01 http://www.neitzvision.com/

01-02 http://www.color-blindness.com/protanopia-red-green-color-blindness/

01-03 http://www.color-blindness.com/deuteranopia-red-green-color-blindness/

01-04 http://www.color-blindness.com/tritanopia-blue-yellow-color-blindness/

01-05 http://discovermagazine.com/2012/jul-aug/06-humans-with-super-human-vision

01-06 http://www.eyemagazine.com/feature/article/ishihara

01-07 http://www.testingcolorvision.com/

01-08 https://www.osha.gov/pls/oshaweb/owadisp.show_document?p_table=INTERPRETATIONS&p_id=24865

01-09 https://www.theguardian.com/news/2000/jun/17/guardianobituaries

01-10 http://www.shikikaku.com/en/shikikaku/

Chapter 2

02-01 http://jfly.iam.u-tokyo.ac.jp/html/manuals/pdf/color_blind.pdf

02-02 http://optional.is/required/2011/06/20/accessible-color-swatches/

02-03 http://colorbrewer2.org/#type=sequential&scheme=BuGn&n=3

02-04 http://cololoracle.org/

Chapter 3

03-01 https://www.w3.org/WAI/intro/wcag.php

03-02 https://www.w3.org/WAI/WCAG20/quickref/#qr-visual-audio-con-trast-contrast

03-03 https://en.wikipedia.org/wiki/Luminance

03-04 https://en.wikipedia.org/wiki/Visual_acuity

03-05 simplyaccessible.com/article/descriptive-alt-attributes/

03-06 http://leaverou.github.io/contrast-ratio/

03-07 https://snook.ca/technical/colour_contrast/colour.html#f-g=33FF33,bg=333333

03-08 http://colorsafe.co/

03-09 http://contrast-finder.tanaguru.com/

03-10 http://wave.webaim.org/

03-11 http://wave.webaim.org/extension/

03-12 https://blog.twitter.com/2012/because-you-have-more-to-show

Chapter 4

04-01 http://content.tfl.gov.uk/standard-tube-map.pdf

04-02 http://content.tfl.gov.uk/bw-large-print-map.pdf

04-03 http://paul-wynne.blogspot.ca/2010/07/london-underground-colour-blind-map-mark.html

04-04 https://abookapart.com/products/design-for-real-life

04-05 http://responsiveimages.org/

Chapter 5

05-01 http://jasonsantamaria.com/articles/the-sweatpants-of-typefaces

Chapter 6

06-01 http://veerle.duoh.com/design/article/all_about_masks_in_photoshop

06-02 https://css-tricks.com/accessible-svgs-high-contrast-mode/

06-03 http://www.bbc.com/news/technology-13054691

06-04 http://www.colourblindawareness.org/

06-05 http://store.steampowered.com/app/12900

06-06 http://www.bbc.com/news/technology-13054691

Conclusion

07-01 http://simplyaccessible.com/article/pragmatism-transcripts/

07-02 https://beyondtellerrand.com/events/duesseldorf-2012/speakers/ mat-marquis

Resources

08-01 https://www.wsj.com/articles/SB10001424052970204349404578100 942150867894

08-02 http://www.colourblindawareness.org/wp-content/uploads/2010/07/ EGA_160711_083.pdf

08-03 http://webaim.org/articles/cognitive/

08-04 http://wearecolorblind.com/

08-05 http://www.color-blindness.com/

08-06 http://www.neitzvision.com/img/research/CV-ReasonForEyes.pdf

08-07 https://www.w3.org/TR/WCAG/

08-08 http://colororacle.org/resources/2007_JennyKelso_ColorDesign_hires.pdf

08-09 http://www.color-blindness.com/color-blindness-tests/

08-10 http://enchroma.com/test/instructions/

08-11 https://dankaminsky.com/dankam/

INDEX

ABOUT A BOOK APART

We cover the emerging and essential topics in web design and development with style, clarity, and above all, brevity—because working designer-developers can't afford to waste time.

COLOPHON

The text is set in FF Yoga and its companion, FF Yoga Sans, both by Xavier Dupré. Headlines and cover are set in Titling Gothic by David Berlow.

ABOUT THE AUTHOR

Geri Coady is a color-obsessed illustrator and designer from Newfoundland, Canada who now lives in Nottingham, UK. A former ad agency art director, she currently works with companies like Simply Accessible, Withings, and Scholastic. She is the author of *Pocket Guide to Colour Accessibility* published by Five Simple Steps, an occasional illustrator for *A List Apart*, and was voted *net Magazine's* Designer of the Year in 2014. Geri has spoken at design and tech events around the world, including Smashing Conference and Future of Web Design.